discard

CHINA

ABDO
Publishing Company

CHINA

by Andrea Pelleschi

Content Consultant
Ken Hammond
Professor of History, New Mexico State University

CREDITS

Published by ABDO Publishing Company, 8000 West 78th Street, Edina, Minnesota 55439. Copyright © 2012 by Abdo Consulting Group, Inc. International copyrights reserved in all countries. No part of this book may be reproduced in any form without written permission from the publisher. The Essential Library™ is a trademark and logo of ABDO Publishing Company.

Printed in the United States of America,
North Mankato, Minnesota
062011
092011

 THIS BOOK CONTAINS AT LEAST 10% RECYCLED MATERIALS.

Editor: Melissa York
Copy Editor: Susan M. Freese
Series design and cover production: Emily Love
Interior production: Kazuko Collins

About the Author: Andrea Pelleschi has been writing and editing children's books for over 12 years, including storybooks, novelty books, graphic novels, and educational books. She has a master's of fine art in creative writing from Emerson College and has taught writing classes for college freshmen. She currently lives in Cincinnati, Ohio, and hopes to travel to China someday to see all of the fantastic sites described in this book.

Library of Congress Cataloging-in-Publication Data
Pelleschi, Andrea, 1962-
  China / by Andrea Pelleschi.
     p. cm. -- (Countries of the world)
  Includes bibliographical references and index.
  ISBN 978-1-61783-107-2
  1. China--Juvenile literature. I. Title.
  DS706.P378 2012
  951--dc23
                              2011019959

Cover: The Great Wall of China

TABLE OF CONTENTS

CHAPTER 1
A VISIT TO CHINA

You eagerly step off the plane in China on your long-awaited vacation. China is the fourth-largest country in the world, and it has so many places to visit that you want to spend months here. You only have a couple of weeks, however.

Your first stop is Beijing, China's capital. Your first impression is that Beijing is not an attractive city, with its widespread pollution, run-down tenements, and heavy traffic. However, Beijing has more treasures to see than any other city in China.

You start out by renting a bike. You soak up the sites on a leisurely ride to the Forbidden City, which is in the center of Beijing. Once you get there, you're mesmerized by the red buildings with their yellow- and gray-tiled roofs. Until the 1920s, this palace was the home of the imperial court and

The Chinese word for China, Zhonghua, means "the Middle Kingdom."

The ornate buildings of the Forbidden City in Beijing are the former home of the Chinese imperial court.

THE FORBIDDEN CITY

The size and grandeur of the Forbidden City are striking. Built in 1420, this enormous palace was home to 24 emperors during the Ming and Qing dynasties. Architect Nguyen An designed the palace along the points of a compass. The major halls face south, because south was considered the direction of imperial rule. The emperor conducted business in the outer court but lived in the inner court, which consists of smaller buildings and gardens. Because the number nine is said to bring good fortune, it is said the palace has 9,999 rooms. And since nine times nine is even luckier, the imperial doors are decorated with 81 brass studs.[1]

forbidden to commoners. Now, it's a museum and a great example of Imperial architecture.

After touring the museum at the Forbidden City, you hop back on your bike and ride past Tiananmen Square, the largest public square in the world. It's home to the mausoleum of Mao Zedong, the founder of the Chinese Communist Party.

From the square, you ride south to the Temple of Heaven complex, which includes a spectacular circular temple called the Hall of Prayer for Good Harvests. Inside, you stare in awe at the round ceiling, which looks like the inside of a kaleidoscope.

The Hall of Prayer for Good Harvests was completed in 1420.

Next on the agenda is the Great Wall of China, north of Beijing. You can choose the Badaling section of the wall, which has guardrails and a cable car. Or if you're feeling more adventurous, you can try another section, with steeper climbs and more spectacular views.

GREAT WALL OF CHINA

The Great Wall of China snakes over mountains, deserts, forests, and plains for approximately 5,500 miles (8,800 km).[2] It begins in the east on the gulf of Bo Hai in the Yellow Sea and extends west to a fort in the Badain Jaran Desert, the southern section of the Gobi Desert. Built to defend against warring nations, the first section of the wall was constructed during the seventh century BCE. It was not until the Qin dynasty in 221 BCE that the various parts of the wall were combined into one giant fortress to protect China's northern border. Succeeding dynasties added sections to the wall, which included not only actual walls but also forts and other defensive structures.

As dusk arrives in the city, you head for the old alleys of Beijing for some dinner and shopping. These *hotungs*—narrow, twisting streets lined by small shops and houses—used to form neighborhoods throughout old Beijing before it was modernized. Today, you can take a rickshaw tour or just stroll past the myriad of shops selling pickles, silk, tea, and Chinese medicine. Hungry? This is also the place to buy an exotic snack of scorpion, shrimp, or squid.

Begun in the seventh century BCE, the Great Wall of China stretches 5,500 miles (8,800 km) across dramatic rolling terrain.

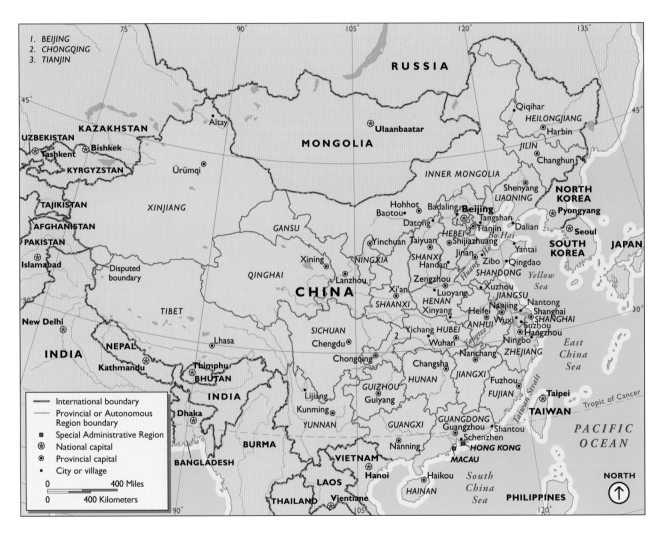

1. BEIJING
2. CHONGQING
3. TIANJIN

Map labels:

RUSSIA

KAZAKHSTAN

UZBEKISTAN
•Tashkent

KYRGYZSTAN
•Bishkek

TAJIKISTAN

AFGHANISTAN

PAKISTAN

Islamabad

New Delhi

INDIA

NEPAL
Kathmandu

BHUTAN
Thimphu

INDIA

BANGLADESH
Dhaka

BURMA

BANGLADESH

Altay•

MONGOLIA

Ulaanbaatar

Ürümqi•

XINJIANG

GANSU

Disputed
boundary

QINGHAI

TIBET

Lhasa•

CHINA

Xining•

NINGXIA

Lanzhou•

Xi'an•

SHAANXI

SICHUAN
Chengdu•

Chongqing•

2

Lijiang•
Kunming•

YUNNAN

GUIZHOU
Guiyang•

GUANGXI

Nanning•

VIETNAM
Hanoi•

LAOS

THAILAND   Vientiane•

INNER MONGOLIA

Qiqihar•
HEILONGJIANG

•Harbin

JILIN
•Changhun

Shenyang•
LIAONING
NORTH
KOREA
•Pyongyang

Hohhot•   Badaling•   Beijing
Baotou•   Tangshan•
Datong•   Tianjin•   Dalian•
HEBEI   Bo Hai
Yinchuan•   Taiyuan•   Shijiazhuang•
SHANXI   Jinan•   Zibo   •Qingdao
Handan•   SHANDONG
Zengzhou•   Huang He
Luoyang•   Xuzhou•
HENAN   JIANGSU   Nantong
Xinyang•   Nanjing•   Shanghai
HUBEI   Heifei•   Wuxi•   SHANGHAI
Yichang•   ANHUI   Suzhou•
Wuhan•   Hangzhou•
Nanchang•   Ningbo•   ZHEJIANG
Changsha•

HUNAN   JIANGXI   Fuzhou•

FUJIAN

GUANGDONG
Guangzhou•   Shantou•
Schenzhen•
HONG KONG
MACAU

Haikou•

HAINAN

SOUTH
KOREA
•Seoul

JAPAN

Yellow
Sea

Yantai•

Yangtze

East
China
Sea

Taipei•

TAIWAN

Taiwan Strait

Tropic of Cancer

PACIFIC
OCEAN

South
China
Sea

PHILIPPINES

NORTH

Legend:

— — — International boundary
——— Provincial or Autonomous
      Region boundary
■ Special Administrative Region
⊛ National capital
◉ Provincial capital
• City or village

0   400 Miles
0   400 Kilometers

Political Boundaries of China

RICH IN ART

Your trip to China wouldn't be complete if you didn't take in some of the nation's traditional artwork. Unfortunately, much of China's art was destroyed or taken to other countries because of war or natural disasters. The Cultural Revolution of the 1960s was particularly damaging to China's art. Communist leader Mao Zedong encouraged citizens to destroy art in the name of progress. Now, China is working hard to restore its cultural treasures.

TERRA-COTTA ARMY

One of the most remarkable sites in China is an entire life-size statue army made of terra-cotta (a reddish-brown clay), located in Xi'an, southwest of Beijing. Emperor Shihuangdi wanted to re-create his empire for the afterlife, so he ordered approximately 700,000 workers to mold thousands of soldiers and place them in his tomb.[3] The tomb is still being excavated, but three pits are open to visitors. Each soldier was made by hand and has distinct facial features. The statues have many intricate details, including studs on the shoes and layers of armor.

You can see traditional calligraphy—the art of elegant writing—on temples, on cave walls, and even on the sides of mountains. Painting is done with an inked brush applied to silk or paper. A poem written in calligraphy often accompanies paintings, creating a harmonious effect.

In addition, you should look for ceramics—particularly porcelain, which was invented by the Chinese—along with sculptures, bronze vessels, and jade carvings. A spectacular example of pottery on a large scale is the life-size terra-cotta army in Xi'an.

ANCIENT AND MODERN

One thing you notice as you tour around China is the mixture of the ancient with the modern. You see farmers using water buffalo to pull their plows in the country, as well as professionals in business suits walking among the skyscrapers of busy Shanghai.

In less than 100 years, China's population has grown from 400 million to 1.3 billion.[4] This growth has helped drive the nation's economy, which has meant more businesses. However, it has also meant that traditional housing has been destroyed to make way for luxury hotels, public transportation, and new highway systems. But the growth process works both ways: Although modern businesses tear down traditional Chinese buildings, they also provide Chinese workers with enough money to honor traditional arts and culture in a way they haven't been able to in many years.

As you tour China, you notice this contrast between the old and the new. Amid the concrete, steel, and neon lights of the cities, songbirds twitter in bamboo cages and pagodas sit majestically on wooded hills— just as they did in ancient times.

SNAPSHOT

Official name: People's Republic of China (Chinese: Zhonghua Renmin Gongheguo)

Capital city: Beijing

Form of government: Communist state

Title of leader: premier (head of government); president (head of state)

Currency: renminbi

Population (July 2011 est.): 1,336,718,015
World rank: 1

Size: 3,705,407 square miles (9,596,961 sq km)
World rank: 4

Language: Standard Chinese or Mandarin, Yue, Wu, Minbei, Minnan, Xiang, Gan, Hakka dialects, minority languages

Official religion: atheism

Per capita GDP (2010, US dollars): $7,400
World rank: 127

CHAPTER 2

GEOGRAPHY: LAND OF CONTRASTS

Located in eastern Asia, China's vast landmass is a study in contrasts: mountains and deserts in the west, subarctic tundra in the north, coastal lowlands in the east, and tropical rain forests in the south. The highest point in the world and the second-lowest point in the world are located in China. Mount Everest, on the border between China and Nepal, towers at 29,035 feet (8,850 m), and the Turfan Depression to the north drops to 508 feet (154 m) below sea level.[1]

China's total landmass is 3,694,983 square miles (9,569,961 sq km), making it the fourth-largest country in the world, only slightly smaller than the United States.[2] China is bordered by Mongolia to the north; Russia and North Korea to the northeast; the Yellow Sea

All of China lies in one time zone.

The Gobi desert stretches across western China and features sand dunes and rock formations.

and the East China Sea to the east; the South China Sea to the southeast; Vietnam, Laos, Burma, India, Bhutan, and Nepal to the south; and Pakistan, Afghanistan, Tajikistan, Kyrgyzstan, and Kazakhstan to the west.

REGIONS AND LAND FORMATIONS

China's topography can be thought of as three steps, or levels, that generally extend from higher elevations in the west to lower elevations in the east. The first step is the Plateau of Tibet. Stretching across both Tibet and China, this region averages an elevation of close to 16,000 feet (4,800 m), making it the highest area of flat terrain in the world.[3] In the Himalayas to the south, on the border between Tibet and Nepal, sits Mount Everest, the highest mountain in the world. Snowmelt from these mountains feeds many rivers in China, including the Huang He, or "Yellow River," and the Yangtze River.

MOUNT EVEREST

Mount Everest, the tallest mountain in the world, straddles the border between China and Nepal in the Himalayas. The Chinese name for the mountain is *Qomolangma*, which is the name of a Tibetan goddess. The English name, *Mount Everest*, comes from an English surveyor who led an expedition team into the Himalayas in the 1840s. However, it took approximately 100 more years before anyone reached the summit of Mount Everest. In 1953, Tenzing Norgay and Sir Edmund Hillary successfully reached the peak. Since then, many expeditions to the top of Everest take place every year, starting from base camps in Nepal and Tibet.

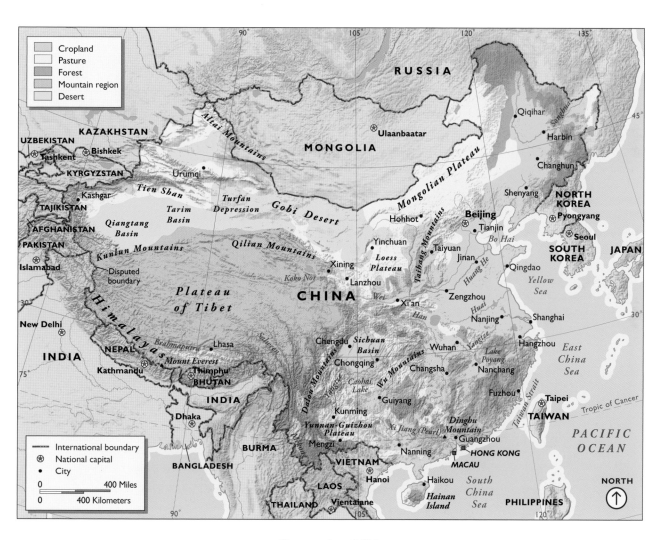

Cropland
Pasture
Forest
Mountain region
Desert

RUSSIA

Qiqihar

Songhua

45°

Harbin

MONGOLIA

Ulaanbaatar

Changhun

KAZAKHSTAN

Altai Mountains

Mongolian Plateau

UZBEKISTAN

Tashkent   Bishkek

KYRGYZSTAN

Ürümqi

Shenyang

NORTH
KOREA

Tien Shan

*Turfan
Depression*

Gobi Desert

Hohhot

Beijing

Pyongyang

Kashgar

Tianjin

TAJIKISTAN

*Tarim
Basin*

Taihang Mountains

Taiyuan

Seoul

SOUTH
KOREA

JAPAN

AFGHANISTAN

*Qiangtang
Basin*

Qilian Mountains

Yinchuan

Bo Hai

Jinan

PAKISTAN

Kunlun Mountains

Xining

*Loess
Plateau*

Lanzhou

Qingdao

*Yellow
Sea*

Islamabad

Disputed
boundary

Koko Nor

CHINA

Wei

Xi'an

Zengzhou

Huang He

30°

New Delhi

*Plateau
of Tibet*

Han

Huai

Nanjing

Shanghai

Himalayas

Brahmaputra

Lhasa

Salween

Chengdu *Sichuan
Basin*

Wuhan

Yangtze

Hangzhou

*East
China
Sea*

INDIA

NEPAL

Mount Everest

Chongqing

*Lake
Poyang*

Nanchang

Kathmandu

Thimphu

Daba Mountains

Wu Mountains

Changsha

BHUTAN

Yangtze

*Caohai
Lake*

Fuzhou

Taipei

Tropic of Cancer

INDIA

Guiyang

TAIWAN

Dhaka

Kunming

*Dinghu
Mountain*

PACIFIC
OCEAN

*Yunnan-Guizhou
Plateau*

Xi Jiang (Pearl)

Guangzhou

BURMA

Mengzi

Nanning

HONG KONG

MACAU

BANGLADESH

VIETNAM

Haikou

*South
China
Sea*

NORTH

LAOS

Hanoi

*Hainan
Island*

PHILIPPINES

THAILAND

Vientaiane

International boundary
National capital
City

0   400 Miles
0   400 Kilometers

Geography of China

SOUTH CHINA KARST

The karst formations in southern China are considered some of the most spectacular examples of humid tropical to subtropical karst landscapes in the world. Karst is formed when limestone dissolves over millions of years, leaving behind unusually shaped and often beautiful landforms. In southern China, the karst covers more than 190,000 square miles (500,000 sq km). It includes the stone forests of Shilin, the cone and tower karsts of Libo, and the Wulong Karst, which boasts giant sinkholes, natural bridges, and caves. Southern China's karst was designated a United Nations Educational, Scientific, and Cultural Organization (UNESCO) World Heritage site in 2007.

The second step consists of a vast arid region in northwest China, north of the Kunlun and Qilian Mountains. This region includes the Turfan depression, Mongolian Plateau, Tarim Basin, and Loess Plateau. The Gobi desert is also located in this area.

The third and lowest step stretches from the eastern area of the second step to the China Sea. Consisting of rolling hills and plains, this area is filled with rivers, canals, and lakes. It is also where most of the population lives.

Overall, China has more than 50,000 rivers.[4] The longest river is the Yangtze, at 3,915 miles (6,300 km), which flows from the Plateau of Tibet to the East China Sea.[5] The Huang He, which is 3,395 miles (5,464 km) long, flows from the Kunlun Mountains to the Bo Hai gulf.[6] Southern China's longest river, the Pearl, is approximately 1,376 miles (2,214 km)

The South China Karst formations were created by the dissolution of limestone over millions of years.

long.[7] The delta of each of these three rivers forms a fertile agricultural region.

CLIMATE AND SEASONS

In general, most of China has a monsoon climate, with a distinct rainy season. In a monsoon climate, winds blow in one direction during one season and shift to blow from another direction in another season. This means that the fall, winter, and spring months are dry in China, but the summer months are rainy.

During the winter, a high-pressure system forms over Mongolia and sends cold, dry winds across the country, keeping China cold and dry. This polar air mass starts in Siberia in the north and crosses the Mongolian Plateau south to northern China, giving this region of the country dry, clear, and sunny winters.

YELLOW RIVER

Archaeologists believe that the Huang He, or Yellow River, is the cradle of Chinese civilization, and many of China's ancient capitals were built along its banks. Starting at the Plateau of Tibet, the Huang He snakes through 20 gorges before it crosses into the relatively flat Loess Plateau. Once there, it picks up loose, yellowish-brown soil, called loess, and becomes muddy. By the time the Huang He leaves the Loess Plateau, it contains eight times the amount of silt it had upon entering. In fact, some experts believe it should be called a mudflow rather than a river. As the Huang He flows over the North China Plain, it deposits this silt onto the land, raising the riverbank by as much as four inches (10 cm) each year.[8]

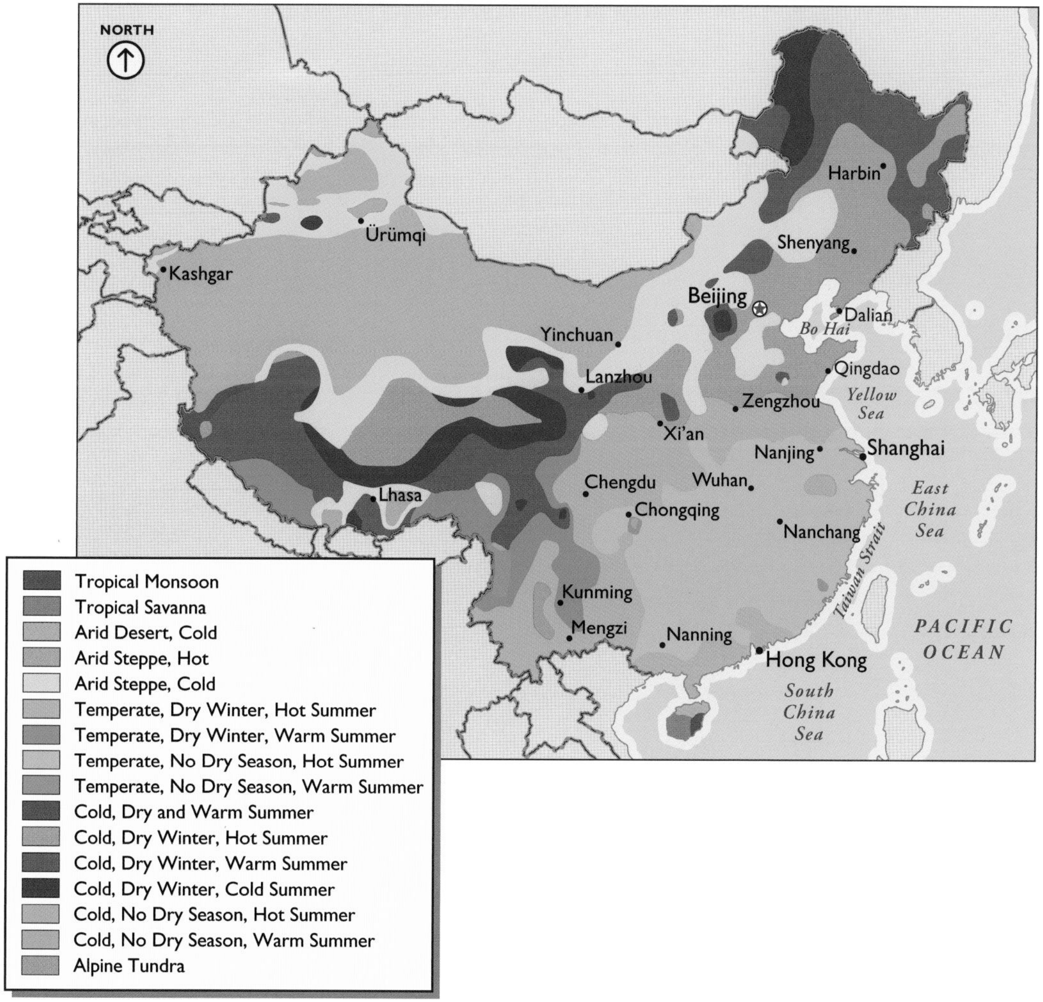
NORTH
Kashgar
Ürümqi
Harbin
Shenyang
Beijing
Dalian
Bo Hai
Yinchuan
Lanzhou
Qingdao
Yellow Sea
Zengzhou
Xi'an
Nanjing
Shanghai
Chengdu
Wuhan
Lhasa
Chongqing
Nanchang
East China Sea
Taiwan Strait
Kunming
Mengzi
Nanning
Hong Kong
PACIFIC OCEAN
South China Sea
Tropical Monsoon
Tropical Savanna
Arid Desert, Cold
Arid Steppe, Hot
Arid Steppe, Cold
Temperate, Dry Winter, Hot Summer
Temperate, Dry Winter, Warm Summer
Temperate, No Dry Season, Hot Summer
Temperate, No Dry Season, Warm Summer
Cold, Dry and Warm Summer
Cold, Dry Winter, Hot Summer
Cold, Dry Winter, Warm Summer
Cold, Dry Winter, Cold Summer
Cold, No Dry Season, Hot Summer
Cold, No Dry Season, Warm Summer
Alpine Tundra

Climate of China

AVERAGE TEMPERATURES AND RAINFALL

Region (City)	Average January Temperature Minimum/Maximum	Average July Temperature Minimum/Maximum	Average Rainfall January/July
Northeast (Beijing)	14/34°F (−10/1°C)	70/88°F (21/31°C)	0.2/9.5 inches (0.4/24.3 cm)
Tibet (Lhasa)	21/45°F (−6/7°C)	48/73°F (9/23°C)	0/4.8 inches (0/12.2 cm)
Central (Shanghai)	34/46°F (1/8°C)	73/90°F (23/32°C)	2/5.8 inches (4.8/14.7cm)
South (Hong Kong)	55/64°F (13/18°C)	79/88°F (26/31°C)	1.3/15 inches (3.3/38.1 cm)
Southwest (Mengzi)	46/68°F (8/20°C)	66/82°F (19/28°C)	0.3/7.7 inches (0.8/19.6 cm)
Western Interior (Kashgar)	12/34°F (−11/−1°C)	68/91°F (20/33°C)	0.6/0.4 inches (1.5/1 cm)
Inner Mongolia (Ürümqi)	−8/12°F (−22/−11°C)	57/82°F (14/28°C)	0.6/0.7 inches (1.5/1.8 cm)[9]

In the spring, low-pressure systems form over northern India and southern China, causing winds to blow from the south. This tropical air mass picks up warm, moist air from the Pacific Ocean and causes rainfall in the summer months. Most of China receives about half of its rain during the summer, with some areas getting as much as 90 percent of their annual rainfall in this season.[10]

CITIES AND PROVINCES

China is divided into 34 geographic regions that fall under control of the government, including 23 provinces, 5 autonomous regions, and 4 municipalities. The provinces include Anhui, Fujian, Gansu, Guangdong, Guizhou, Hainan, Hebei, Heilongjiang, Henan, Hubei, Hunan, Jiangsu, Jiangxi, Jilin, Liaoning, Qinghai, Shaanxi, Shandong, Shanxi, Sichuan, Yunnan, and Zhejiang. China counts Taiwan among its provinces, although Taiwan considers itself to be a separate country.

The autonomous regions are large areas in which the government has limited control over the minority populations who live there. These regions include Guangxi, Nei Mongol, Ningxia, Xinjiang Uygur, and Xizang (Tibet).

Several municipalities, along with their counties, have the same level of governmental control as provinces. They include Beijing (the national capital), Chongqing, Shanghai, and Tianjin.

Hong Kong and Macau are special administrative regions. Hong Kong was a British colony and Macau was a Portuguese colony until China took them over in the late 1990s. To maintain Hong Kong and Macau's existing economic, social, and legal systems, China established them as special administrative regions rather than as provinces.

SHANGHAI

In the early part of its history, Shanghai was a simple fishing village, but by the eighteenth century, it had become a major port for smuggling drugs—especially opium. In the nineteenth century, the French and British settled there, modernizing and expanding the city until it became the largest port in Asia. In the 1920s, Shanghai was known as the "Paris of the Orient," but it was also known for opium smuggling and prostitution. The Chinese Communist Party cleaned up much of the city's illegal activity. Then in the 1990s, Shanghai began growing economically. It reversed its long period of decline and became China's largest trading center. Recently, miles of new highways, thousands of skyscrapers, and the world's fastest train have been built there.

Shanghai is one of China's major cities.

CHAPTER 3

ANIMALS AND NATURE: DIVERSITY OF LIFE

Because of China's varied topography and climate, its wildlife is extremely diverse. China is home to at least 500 species of mammals, 1,300 species of birds, 400 species of reptiles, and 300 species of amphibians.[1]

Mammals reside all over China. In Tibet's mountains and valleys, chiru (a type of antelope), wild ass, wild sheep, goats, wolves, and snow leopards all make their homes. In the foothills of the Himalayas live China's iconic giant pandas, as well as red pandas, Asiatic black bears, leopards, golden takin (a type of antelope), argali sheep, deer, squirrels, badgers, martens, and macaque (a type of monkey known for grabbing food from unsuspecting tourists). Near Siberia live reindeer, moose, musk deer, bears, sables, and Manchurian tigers (also known as Siberian

China's unofficial national animal, the panda, relies on bamboo for food.

ENDANGERED SPECIES IN CHINA

According to the International Union for Conservation of Nature (IUCN), China is home to the following numbers of species that are categorized by the organization as Critically Endangered, Endangered, or Vulnerable:

Mammals	74
Birds	85
Reptiles	31
Amphibians	87
Fishes	97
Mollusks	8
Other Invertebrates	24
Plants	453
Total	859[3]

tigers). Asiatic elephants, Indochinese tigers, and snub-nosed monkeys are found in the rain forests of the south. A type of freshwater dolphin (one of the few found in the world) swims in the Yangtze River, and the rare gibbon (a small ape) is found on the island of Hainan.

In addition, China has a wide variety of birds, including 62 species of pheasants, 36 species of laughing thrushes, nine species of cranes, and many kinds of parrotbills and jays.[2] Lake Koko Nor, a salt lake in northwestern China, is a breeding ground for cranes, geese, sandpipers, and other birds. In Lake Poyang and areas flooded by the Yangtze River live waterfowl such as ducks,

Macaques live in the thick forests in the Qionglai Mountains.

WOLONG NATURE RESERVE

The Wolong Nature Reserve is located between the Sichuan Basin and the Plateau of Tibet. Founded in 1963, this conservation area supports a wide variety of plants and animals, including panthers, macaques, white-lipped deer, takins, and snow leopards. The giant panda, however, is the most famous of the animals that live in Wolong, which is the largest of China's 16 panda conservation reserves. In the Giant Panda Breeding Center, scientists artificially breed and raise more pandas than anywhere else in the world.

geese, herons, and egrets. Black-necked cranes, storks, and other waterfowl spend the winter in the Caohai Lake wetlands near Guizhou Province. In the Mai Po Marsh in Hong Kong, migratory waterfowl and waders, such as the spoon-billed sandpiper, make their home. The Wolong Nature Reserve hosts golden, blood, eared, and kalij pheasants, as well as Chinese monal, partridges, grandala, and the lammergeier, a bearded vulture with a wingspan of more than six and one-half feet (2 m).

Reptiles and amphibians live in the wetlands, rivers, and lakes throughout China, including more than 300 species of frogs, salamanders, and snakes.[4] The Chinese alligator, also known as the "muddy dragon," is the smallest crocodile in the world, measuring only six and one-half feet (2 m). The giant salamander lives in the mountains of southwestern China. It is the world's largest amphibian and measures more than three feet (1 m) long. In addition, China is home to a wide variety of carp and catfish.

The lammergeier lives in mountainous areas.

GIANT PANDA

The giant panda's habitat has been dramatically reduced by several factors, including a growing human population and development for agriculture, bamboo harvesting, construction, and mining. Only a few isolated patches of forest remain available to the giant panda, and researchers estimate that only 1,600 pandas are left in the wild.[10] Conservation efforts have included increasing nature preserves, creating green corridors, and preventing illegal harvesting of bamboo.

waterway in the world, but today, it is largely impassable. To address the problem of desertification, the Chinese government has implemented new laws that limit the number of livestock allowed in a single area. However, experts worry these laws are too little and too late.

Development has also taken away important habitats for many endangered species, including the giant panda. To combat this loss of habitat, China has created more than 2,000 protected areas, including nature reserves, forest parks, scenic areas, and nonhunting areas.[8] The first area was established in 1956 on Dinghu Mountain in Guangdong Province. Today, about 15 percent of the country's land has been set aside for conservation.[9]

Air pollution lingers over Chinese cities.

Pollution is another serious environmental problem in China. Water pollution from sewage and industrial waste has contaminated rivers and lakes, causing most of China to experience water shortages. And because the nation relies on coal as its main fuel for creating power, China has become one of the highest emitters of greenhouse gases and sulfur dioxide in the world. This air pollution has led to formation of clouds containing acid rain, which damages forests and crops when it falls.

ENVIRONMENTAL FACTS

Land	China loses 1,158 square miles (2,000 sq km) of land each year to desertification.
	Forty percent of the land in China is eroding or becoming less fertile.
Water	Seventy percent of China experiences water shortages.
	Three-fourths of all rivers in China have water that is too polluted for drinking or fishing.
Air	China is the second-highest creator of greenhouse gases in the world and the highest emitter of sulfur dioxide.
	Approximately 600,000 Chinese people are expected to die from air pollution each year until 2020.[11]

Air pollution has also caused respiratory problems for many people who live in cities.

China is looking for alternate sources of fuel and imposing a tax on high-sulfur coal to help reduce air pollution. In addition, China is developing forms of green energy, including solar power and electric cars.

China has 66 critically endangered animal species.

CHAPTER 4

HISTORY: THE OLDEST CIVILIZATION

China is home to what is likely the longest continuous civilization in the world. Remains of the human ancestor *Homo erectus* believed to be 2 million years old were found in present-day Shaanxi and Yunnan Provinces. By 5000 BCE, an agricultural society had developed in three areas of China: the middle Huang He and Wei River valleys, the lower Yangtze River, and the southeastern coast.

The first people ancient Chinese historians wrote about were the Xia, who would have existed from the late Neolithic period to the Bronze Age. Some evidence suggests the Xia farmed the land, made pottery, and used bronze weapons, but no written records survive from this time and scientists are unsure of the dynasty's existence.

After the Xia came the Shang, known as China's first dynasty, which began in approximately 1600 BCE. Shang kings inherited their positions

The bronze handle of a cane remains from the time of the Shang, China's first dynasty.

from their fathers and had absolute power, including some influence in heaven. When the kings died, they were buried with sacrificial slaves and captives from wars. The Shang were the first group in China to use writing.

In the eleventh century BCE, the Shang were defeated by the Zhou, a seminomadic tribe that had settled in the Wei River valley. The Zhou developed a feudal system of government, in which relatives of the Zhou king became lords over people living in states within the kingdom. The Zhou kings were thought to be "Sons of Heaven" with divine rights. All land in the kingdom belonged to the king and was held by others as gifts.

At the end of the Zhou dynasty came the Warring States period (475–221 BCE), during which the feudal states battled for domination. This period is also referred to as the Classical era, because philosophers developed Confucianism, Taoism, and Legalism at that time. In addition, literature flourished during this era, and scholars wrote down a system of laws.

IMPERIAL DYNASTIES

In 221 BCE, Emperor Shihuangdi founded the Qin dynasty. He divided the empire into provinces, which became the basis for China's later governments, and he standardized language, weights, measures, and money. To protect the empire from the nomadic people to the north, the Qin emperor created the first Great Wall of China. When he died, he was buried in Xi'an with at least 7,000 life-size terra-cotta warriors.

Emperor Shihuangdi's terra-cotta warriors

CONQUEST AND RESTORATION

In 1211, Genghis Khan and the Mongols invaded China from the north. This nomadic group of people had already conquered Russia and central Asia. Genghis Khan normally slaughtered the people he conquered, but after learning about Chinese silk, silver, and grain, he chose to tax the Chinese instead.

Genghis Kahn's grandson, Kublai Khan, expanded his kingdom into southern China and controlled all of China, Korea, Tibet, and Burma by 1279, ending the Song dynasty. He called his dynasty the Yüan and moved the capital to Beijing. During his reign, people from all over the world—including artisans, ambassadors, and merchants—traveled to Beijing. Despite the Mongolian embrace of

GENGHIS KHAN

Genghis Khan was born in Mongolia in 1162 with the name Temujin. In 1206, he became the Genghis Khan, or "universal king." He united the warring factions in Mongolia and built an army of 200,000 soldiers. Part of his success came from the supply of skilled Mongolian cavalrymen available to him. They were known for their small and sturdy horses, heavy armor, and ability to live off the land with no other supplies. By the time of Genghis Khan's death in 1227, he had conquered parts of Asia and China, creating one of the largest empires in history.

Genghis Khan and the Mongols conquered much of Asia.

Chinese culture, many Chinese people refused to accept Mongolian rule. Rebellions led by a peasant named Zhu Chongba forced the Mongols to retreat north of the Great Wall.

In 1368, Zhu Chongba created the Ming dynasty and established the capital in Nanjing. After naming himself the Hongwu emperor, he changed the structure of the government to give himself more power than previous emperors.

Shortly after Hongwu died, the Yongle emperor seized power in 1403. The Yongle emperor was Hongwu's son, but he had not been named heir. He moved the capital to Beijing, and he rebuilt the imperial palace and the Forbidden City. China opened up to the West during this time, when the Yongle emperor sent ocean-going vessels on diplomatic missions to the East Indies, the Persian Gulf, and the coast of eastern Africa. In turn, Europeans began trading with China, beginning with the Portuguese and followed by the Dutch, the Spanish, and the British.

During the late Ming dynasty, the Great Wall was strengthened and extended, making it largely the wall that it is today. The Ming dynasty fell apart in 1644 due to internal power struggles and rebellions.

OPENING UP TO THE WEST

In 1644, the Manchu invaded China from the northeast and began the Qing dynasty. The Qing adopted the Ming style of government and established a Chinese and a Manchu post for each governmental position.

RISE OF COMMUNISM

The early 1900s was a period of revolution and civil war in China. Anti-Manchu sentiment led to the formation of the Nationalist Party by Sun Yat-sen, who is considered the father of modern China. He wanted to lead China into becoming a more democratic and socialist country. He was influential in the revolution of 1911, which led Puyi to step down on February 12, 1912, marking the end of the Qing dynasty. Through the next several years, a series of warlords fought for control of the government.

Mao Zedong was born on December 26, 1893.

In 1921, the Chinese Communist Party (CCP) was formed and joined the Nationalists in fighting the warlords. Sun Yat-sen died in 1925 and Chiang Kai-shek became leader of the Nationalists. Several years later, Chiang Kai-shek betrayed the CCP and slaughtered many Communist workers. He set up a government in Nanjing and drove Mao Zedong, the leader of the CCP, into the countryside.

In 1930, Mao formed the Jiangxi Soviet in the mountains and worked to improve conditions for peasants by redistributing land to them. When Chiang Kai-shek and the Nationalist army drove Mao and the CCP out of their mountain retreat 1934, Mao began walking across China with other Communist revolutionaries. Over the next year, they walked 6,000 miles (10,000 km) in what became known as the Long March. Approximately 86,000 people began the march, but only 8,000 made it to Shaanxi Province, the final destination.[2]

Mao Zedong

In 1949, Mao became chairman of the newly formed Zhonghua Renmin Gongheguo, or People's Republic of China, in Beijing. Because of his efforts at land reform, people throughout China supported him. Chiang Kai-shek was forced to escape to Taiwan, where he established a Nationalist government.

Mao set about improving political and economic conditions in China, but his reforms often made conditions worse for the Chinese. With his Hundred Flowers Campaign, he tried to encourage freedom of expression, but when he was criticized, he banished intellectuals to the countryside. During the Great Leap Forward, he ordered communities to cook food collectively so women could spend more time on their jobs instead of cooking for their families. However, unrealistic expectations and natural disasters led to a devastating famine. In 1966, Mao instituted the Cultural Revolution, a period of upheaval that spanned ten years. But instead of

CULTURAL REVOLUTION

In 1966, Mao Zedong set out to create a new educational system in China that would eliminate class differences and simultaneously boost his own status. He enlisted the aid of students in the newly formed Red Guard to lead this revolution. Schools were shut down and writers and artists were persecuted or killed. Fear led many people to accuse family members and neighbors of not following Mao's doctrine. By the time the revolution ended in 1976 with Mao's death, large numbers of people had died from beatings, executions, and lack of medical treatment.

Tiananmen Square has been the site of many protests and rallies over the years.

eliminating the differences between classes as intended, the movement caused widespread fear, violence, and death.

After Mao's death in 1976, Deng Xiaoping rose to power. He returned land to the peasants and put in place economic reforms. During the 1980s and 1990s, China's economy improved dramatically to become one of the largest in the world. However, freedom of expression suffered, culminating in an act of violence in 1989 at Tiananmen Square in which student protesters were shot by government forces.

Tiananmen Square covers 100 acres (40.5 ha).

As China moved into the twenty-first century, it continued to expand its economy. It also continued to struggle with human rights issues, environmental problems, and running a socialist country with capitalist characteristics.

CHAPTER 5

PEOPLE: PROUD TRADITIONS

Home to more than 1.3 billion people, China is the world's most populous country.[1] Though the country encompasses a large area, most of its population is concentrated in the plains, the coastline, and south-central China.

Although it has four times the population of the United States, China only has about three-fourths as much arable land.[2] This makes it hard for China to feed all of its people. To control the population, the Chinese government instituted a mandatory family-planning law in 1979, penalizing families that have more than one child. China has the lowest birthrate of any developing country, and its population may start declining by the middle of the twenty-first century.

China has one of the world's largest urban populations with nearly 200 cities each containing more than one million people.

DEMOGRAPHICS

Total population	1,336,718,015
Median age	35.5 years
Male life expectancy	72.68 years
Female life expectancy	76.94 years
Population growth rate	0.493 %
Fertility rate	1.54 children born/woman
Death rate	7.03 deaths/1,000 population
Gender ratio at birth	1.133 males to 1 female[6]

In 2007, China had 570 cities, 170 of them with populations over a million people.[3] Approximately 47 percent of the total population lives in cities.[4] During the 1970s, it was illegal for a family living in the country to move to the city without approval. Lately, this regulation has been relaxed because of the need for workers to take undesirable, low-paying jobs, and so migration to the cities has increased. Called the "floating population," about 100 million people continue to live on farms yet travel to industrial urban areas to work at low pay rates.[5]

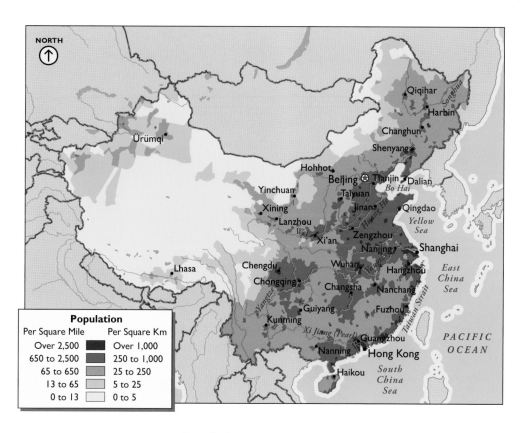

Population		
Per Square Mile		Per Square Km
Over 2,500		Over 1,000
650 to 2,500		250 to 1,000
65 to 650		25 to 250
13 to 65		5 to 25
0 to 13		0 to 5

Population Density of China

ETHNIC GROUPS

Ethnically, China is a very homogeneous country. The Han Chinese make up close to 92 percent of the population, or about 1.2 billion people.[7]

The people of China are statistically very homogenous, but an array of different ethnicities make up a small percentage of the population.

About three-fourths of the Han speak Mandarin, a form of Chinese, and one-quarter speak different dialects.[8] Written Mandarin is uniform, but there are several very different spoken versions heard in different regions of the country.

There are 55 minority groups in China, comprising a relatively small 8 percent of the population. Minority groups live on 60 percent of the land, mostly in autonomous regions along China's borders.[9]

The Zhuang are the largest minority population and live mainly in Guangxi in the south. Their language and culture are related to the Thai people, and they are known for their rice terraces.

The Mongols live in Inner Mongolia in the north. They share the language and culture—including the nomadic past—of the Mongolians who once formed the Yüan dynasty. The Mongols practice Tibetan Buddhism.

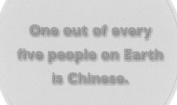

One out of every five people on Earth is Chinese.

The Manchu are known for conquering China and forming the Qing dynasty, which ended in 1912. Today, descendents reside in Xinjiang and speak dialects of Manchu, a language related to Mongolian.

The Tibetans live in Tibet and also throughout China. They practice Tibetan Buddhism and speak Tibetan, a language distantly related to other Chinese languages but written with an adapted ancient Indian script.

The Uighurs are a Muslim Turkic people who live in Xinjiang. They share a language, religion, and culture with the Uzbeks of central Asia.

ETHNIC POPULATIONS[10]

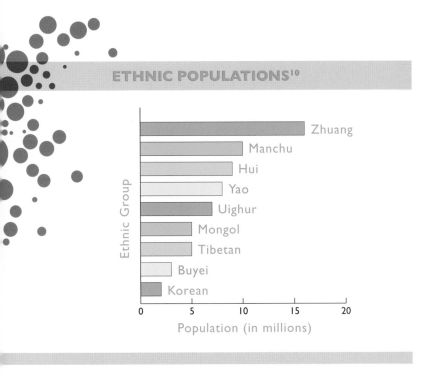

Ethnic Group

- Zhuang
- Manchu
- Hui
- Yao
- Uighur
- Mongol
- Tibetan
- Buyei
- Korean

Population (in millions)
0 5 10 15 20

The Hui descended from Muslims of central Asia and the Middle East. They live in the northwest in Gansu and Ningxia and have also settled throughout China. Also in the northwest lives a population of Koreans, who are concentrated along the North Korean border.

A mixture of ethnic minorities live in Yunnan Province in the south: the Buyei, Tai, Yao, and Naxi. They speak a language similar to Thai and Vietnamese. No single group dominates the region.

LANGUAGE

The blanket term "Chinese language" includes Mandarin, as well as seven other varieties: Cantonese, Shanghaiese, Fuzhou, Hokkien-Taiwanese, Xiang, Gan, and Hakka. Subtypes of these varieties and unique minority languages are spoken in China as well.

Spoken Chinese varies, but written Chinese is uniform.

The official language of China is Mandarin as it is spoken in Beijing, which is called *Putonghua*, or "common speech." The varieties of Chinese are related somewhat in the way Romance languages such as Spanish and Italian are related—they are similar, but a native speaker of one language will not automatically understand the others. However, all of these variations share the same written language—speakers simply pronounce the same written characters differently. In the twentieth century, the government began a successful campaign to teach Putonghua as a second language to people around the country.

Chinese calligraphy has six types: seal script, clerical, regular, cursive, semicursive, and simplified.

The Chinese language is part of the Sino-Tibetan group of languages, which includes Tibetan, Burmese, and other languages from southwestern and southeastern Asia. However, Chinese is not related to Japanese, Korean, or Mongolian, despite the close proximity of these countries. Any similarity between written Japanese and written Chinese exists because the Japanese developed their written language from the Chinese, who began writing centuries before peoples in other Asian countries.

Chinese has a simple grammatical structure of subject-verb-object, which is similar to English. Chinese does not use articles (*a*, *an*, *the*), verbs do not show tense, and no distinction is made between singular and plural nouns. (For example, the Chinese word *ma* can mean one horse or several horses.)

Spoken Chinese is complicated because its meaning changes with the tone of the speaker's voice. Chinese has 400 syllables, and each syllable can be spoken using a different tone or inflection that changes the meaning of the word. The four tones include starting high and staying level, starting high and rising even higher, starting low and then dropping and rising again, and starting high and falling quickly.

Written Chinese is much harder to learn than spoken Chinese because it uses characters rather than an alphabet. Instead of learning a couple dozen letters, as in English and many other Western languages, a person needs to learn approximately 3,000 characters to function in everyday Chinese society. A well-educated person may need to learn more than 5,000 characters.[11]

Each Chinese character represents a syllable or an idea, so a word comprises either a single character or a combination of two or more characters. Characters are combinations of meanings plus sounds. Today, new words are formed by combining existing characters.

YOU SAY IT!

English	Pinyin
Hello	ní hǎo (knee how)
Good-bye	Zài jiàn (zih gee'ehn)
Excuse me	Duí bu qǐ (dway boo chee)
Thank you	Xiè xiè (sheh sheh)

In 1954, the Committee for Reforming the Chinese Language simplified 2,200 of the characters to make the language more accessible. Then in 1958, the government created pinyin, a form of Chinese that uses a Roman alphabet instead of characters. Pinyin has since become the international standard for writing Chinese, but it is not commonly used by the Chinese people.

RELIGION

Since the Cultural Revolution in the 1960s, China has seen a revival of religion among its people. Traditional Chinese practices including Buddhism, Taoism, and ancestor worship have increased in popularity again, and newer faiths such as Christianity are gaining followers.

Taoism is a religion and a philosophy that focuses on accepting what happens naturally. Tao is a spirit—the divine power of nature and the order behind all life. Humans cannot sense Tao, because it exists outside their ability to imagine it. The only way to know Tao is to experience it through a spiritual vision or awakening. According to this religion, people should order their lives according to Tao to keep harmony with the universe. People who practice Taoism strive for immortality in the afterlife. They also study yin and yang and practice martial arts such as Tai Chi.

Large Buddha sculptures erected as shrines similar to this one in Hong Kong are a common sight across China.

This Shanghai statue honors Confucius, one of the founders of Chinese philosophy.

CHAPTER 6

CULTURE: A RICH HERITAGE

Calligraphy, or the art of handwriting, is considered the highest art form in China. Legend says that it was created by artist Cangjie after he saw the tracks of birds and animals in the snow. Both beautiful and practical, calligraphy uses the "four treasures of the scholar's study," which are paper, ink, brush, and an ink stone (to mix the ink).[1] Calligraphy was first used on bone, brass, and stone in ancient China and eventually applied to silk and paper, where it developed a more fluid style.

Painting also uses the "four treasures." As in calligraphy, the thickness and tone of the brush line is the most important aspect of painting. The goal of traditional Chinese painting is not to achieve an exact likeness of a subject but rather to represent its inner spirit. Traditional subjects include landscapes, people, birds, flowers, religious figures, and bamboo.

Brushstrokes are an important aspect of traditional Chinese painting.

Porcelain is China's most famous form of pottery. Made from a type of white clay, porcelain is fired using a high temperature to create a pure white material that is translucent and very hard. The popular blue-and-white porcelain, developed during the Ming dynasty, is made by painting cobalt blue glaze over clay and then covering the entire piece with a transparent glaze. Chinese porcelain became so prized all over the world that it became known as "Chinaware." Today, fancy dinnerware is simply called "china."

Other significant Chinese art forms include sculpture, bronze vessels, jade carvings, lacquer carvings, and cloisonné (enamel-covered metal). In addition, the Chinese invention of silk raised textiles to an art form and gave China a thriving export business for centuries.

SILK

Approximately 6,000 years ago, the Chinese learned to turn cocoons from mulberry-eating moths into a strong and beautiful cloth. Today, silkworms are bred on farms and taken to factories, where they are fed leaves until they grow fat and enter the pupae stage. At that point, they excrete a clear liquid and weave it into a cocoon. Workers soak the cocoons to soften and separate the strands, which kills the pupae. It takes six or seven cocoons to create a thread strong enough to be woven into cloth.

MUSIC

Traditional Chinese music is based on ancient poetry and dates back to the Shang dynasty. In Chinese music,

Chinese silk making dates back thousands of years.

BEIJING OPERA

Beijing opera uses bold makeup, bright costumes, and exciting acrobatics to tell its stories. Symbolism is extremely important. For example, the color of a character's face paint gives the audience clues about his or her personality: red is for loyalty, green for bravery, and purple for fairness. Higher ranking characters have increasingly elaborate headdresses. Performers speak and sing, while percussive instruments including gongs, drums, and clappers accompany them, often contributing to the emotion of a scene.

tone is more important than melody, and the musical scale is not the same as the one used in Western music. Traditional instruments include a two-stringed fiddle, a four-stringed banjo, a two-stringed viola, a vertical flute, a horizontal flute, a zither, and a trumpet. Today, modern popular music can be heard throughout China, including rock, metal, and punk.

There are more than 300 types of opera in China, including Beijing, Yue, and Kunqu.[2] Chinese opera developed during the Song dynasty, when traveling entertainers performed in teahouses for people of the working class. These operas told stories rooted in legends and folklore. In the nineteenth century, the Beijing opera became popular for imperial families as well as the general public.

Operas in China tell stories of legends and folklore through lively costume, makeup, and songs.

HOLIDAYS AND FESTIVALS

The biggest festival in China is the Spring Festival, or Chinese New Year, which is celebrated across 15 days in the winter. Families put up decorations, exchange gifts, and prepare special foods. Fireworks provide a spectacular climax to the festival. The Lantern Festival comes right after the Chinese New Year. At this time, children display lanterns that are often in the shapes of animals.

Other festivals occur throughout the rest of the year, including dragon boat races in June, Ghost Month in August (when ghosts are believed to walk among the living), and the birthday of Confucius in September. A national holiday occurs on October 1 to celebrate the anniversary of the founding of the People's Republic of China.

FOOD

In ancient China, foods were designed to tempt a departing soul back into its body. Meals were prepared to satisfy the five sensations of taste: sweetness, sourness, pungency or hotness, bitterness, and saltiness. Today, traditional Chinese meals feature a grain, such as rice or noodles, served with vegetables, a soy product such as tofu, and sometimes meat or fish.

Meals should be designed to appeal to all senses and to blend yin and yang, thus achieving balance and harmony. For instance, bland dishes should be served with strongly flavored dishes, and crisp foods should be served with soft foods. Moist and soft foods, such as fruits and vegetables,

Eaten with chopsticks, traditional Chinese meals aim to appeal to all senses with a balance of textures and flavors.

TEA

Some evidence suggests China was the first country to cultivate tea, beginning approximately 5,000 years ago. Today, tea is China's national drink. Grown in the warm and wet southern climate, the most common types of tea are black, green, and oolong. Differences in appearance and taste are due to the area in which the tea was grown and the type of fermentation used to process the leaves. Traditionally, tea is drunk without milk, sugar, or lemon. However, in the northwestern Muslim areas of China, it is drunk with sugar, and in Tibet, it is drunk with butter.

are considered yin foods and provide coolness. Hot and spicy foods are considered yang foods and provide warmth.

Hot and spicy Sichuan dishes are one example of China's many distinctive regional cooking styles. Northern cuisine features steamed bread and noodles. Southern-style stir-fried cooking uses a large variety of ingredients, including seafood, chicken, and pork.

SPORTS

Archaeologists have found evidence that sports began in China at least 4,000 years ago. The ancient Chinese practiced a version of modern-day Tai Chi, a type of martial art that combines breathing exercises with movement. In the Tang dynasty, aristocrats played polo, a ball-and-mallet game played on horseback. People of the Song dynasty played games that involved kicking a ball down a field, not unlike modern soccer. In the Yüan dynasty, a version of golf became popular. In the twentieth century, the Chinese began competing in sporting events around the world, including the Olympic Games. By the 1980s, hundreds of Chinese participated in each Summer Olympics, taking medals in badminton, diving, gymnastics, swimming, table tennis, and volleyball, among other sports. In 2003, the international football (soccer) association recognized China as the birthplace of soccer. And in 2008, Beijing hosted the Summer Olympics.

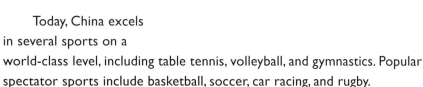

KUNG FU

China's combative martial art is called kung fu, which means "skill." China has a large number of fighting styles, with colorful names such as Drunken Boxing and Praying Mantis Fist. There are two basic forms of kung fu: internal and external. Internal forms use evasion and softness to put an attacker out of balance. These forms emphasize internal power, or chi. External forms use strength and power to overwhelm an attacker. Weapons include spears, broadswords, poles, and even everyday objects such as umbrellas and stools.

Today, China excels in several sports on a world-class level, including table tennis, volleyball, and gymnastics. Popular spectator sports include basketball, soccer, car racing, and rugby.

LITERATURE

Historically, two forms of literature developed in China: classical and vernacular. The classical genre encompasses poetry, prose and historical writing, and philosophical texts. The philosophical texts are mostly based on the writings of Confucius and composed in ancient Chinese, which meant they were inaccessible to the general public. Classical literature was used to test candidates on civil service exams and became the backbone of the educational system. Important classical texts include the *Yijing* or *I Ching* (*The Book of Changes*), China's oldest text, which might date to the twelfth century BCE; *Lunyu* (*The Analects*), a collection of Confucius's ideas written in approximately 500 BCE; and the *Daodejing* (*Classic of the Way of Power*), a book outlining Taoist doctrine that scholars date anywhere from the eighth to the third century BCE.

The vernacular form of literature became popular during the Ming dynasty (1368–1644 CE). Works in this genre, written in everyday language, were read more for entertainment than for education. These texts told stories about ordinary life and laid the foundation for the modern novel.

The oldest collection of Chinese poetry is the *Book of Songs* from the sixth century BCE. It includes more than 300 poems that express ideas about love, marriage, war, hunting, and sacrifice.[3] The Tang dynasty (618–907 CE) is considered the golden age of Chinese poetry, and Lu Bai and Du Fu are considered the greatest poets from that period.

CINEMA

The first Chinese film was made in 1905, but a true Chinese film industry did not develop until the late 1910s. Early Chinese film reached its peak in the 1930s in Shanghai but was cut off in 1949 when the Communist

> Chinese can be written using six different systems of calligraphy.

Chinese martial arts actors Jet Li and Jackie Chan
promoting a kung fu film

Party took power. Changes under the new regime caused filmmakers, along with other artists, to flee to Taiwan and Hong Kong, where they built new local film industries.

China has the third-largest film industry in the world, after the United States and India.

Filmmaking declined during Mao Zedong's regime as the Chinese Communist Party forced filmmakers to follow rigid political rules. After Mao's death in 1976, filmmakers enjoyed more freedom. By the 1980s and 1990s, many films had gained critical and commercial success in China and abroad, such as *House of Flying Daggers*. Actors such as Jet Li and Chow Yun Fat have also become successful—not just in Chinese films but in US films as well. Jackie Chan became a sensation in China and abroad with his comedic kung fu films, in which he performed all of his own often-dangerous stunts.

ARCHITECTURE

Facing centuries of wars and natural disasters, very few buildings have been preserved from ancient times. Chinese culture has had the expectation that buildings will not last forever. If a building needed to be repaired or rebuilt, it was often torn down and a new one was constructed in its place.

Even so, evidence shows that imperial and religious buildings in China have followed the same basic pattern for the past 2,000 years. A raised platform formed the foundation for the building. Post-and-beam timber pillars were added on the platform and framed the building. A roof sat on the pillars, supported by roof ridges. Building complexes, such as temples, were laid out with a front gate, courtyards, and a series of halls running from north to south. Halls were large buildings made of wood and painted in bright colors. Clay tile roofs had large overhanging eaves that curved upward.

The Chinese also constructed pavilions, pagodas, and pailous. A pavilion is a multistory building that usually houses an important collection, such as books. A pagoda is a religious building that was originally designed to hold statues. A pailou is an ornamental archway that stands at a crossroads, temple, tomb, or bridge.

GARDENS

Traditional Chinese gardens use rocks, water, plants, and architecture to create a picture and a serene environment. They are designed according to the Taoist philosophy that meditation can lead to enlightenment.

When designing a Chinese garden, every element is important. Limestone and yellow rocks mimic mountains and caves. Water makes a small garden look larger and balances the rocks. Plants are used carefully based on their symbolism. For instance, lotus flowers symbolize purity, bamboo stands for resolve, and pine means longevity. Pavilions and halls provide places for meditation and shelter.

Today, some of the tallest buildings in the world are in China, such as the Shanghai Financial Center at 1,614 feet (492 m) and the Nanjing Greenland Financial Center at 1,500 feet (457 m).[4] Other famous buildings include two unusual structures that push the boundaries of architectural design. The National Olympic Sports Center, referred to as the "Bird's Nest," was built for the 2008 Olympics in Beijing. Even though it resembles a bird's nest with its steel, sticklike structure, its design was inspired by pottery in Beijing markets. The National Center for Performing Arts, known as the "Egg," is built of titanium and glass.

The 2008 Olympics were the most expensive in history to date.

The National Olympic Sports Center, Beijing

CHAPTER 7
POLITICS: A MULTILAYERED SYSTEM

China is a Communist country, which means its economy is largely controlled by the national government. China is focused on becoming the largest economy in the world within the next couple of decades, and in pursuit of this goal, it is moving away from government-owned businesses and toward privately owned businesses. This shift is improving the standard of living for many

Flag of China

COMMUNISM

In 1843, German philosopher Karl Marx developed a new view of capitalism. He believed the nature of capitalism allowed property-owning elites to exploit the working class. He called for the overthrow of capitalism and the establishment of an economic and political system that would ensure the workers who produced wealth would share equally in the fruits of their labor. Marx outlined his beliefs in the *Manifesto of the Communist Party*, which he wrote in 1848 with Friedrich Engels. Eventually, the term *communism* came to mean a government that is ruled by a single party with no opposition and an economy in which the state controls all property, wages, and production. China is one of the few Communist countries in existence today.

Chinese, helping them recover from the damaging policies of Mao Zedong during the 1960s and 1970s. But it is also causing a range of other problems.

Many of the problems involve the rural peasant class of China. Migrant workers who move from the countryside to the cities work for low pay, live in poor housing, and have few social services. There is already an income gap between city and rural workers—income is estimated at $1,382 per capita for urban workers but only $565 for rural ones—and this gap may grow as more workers move to the cities.[1] Back home, peasants have to contend with the actions of local governments. These governments take peasants' land to build factories and roads, paying them well below the actual value of their property, and tax peasants at high rates.

China must also work around its lack of fertile farmland. The country has only a small amount of arable land because of its vast deserts and mountains, and this land is being used for development or lost to encroaching deserts. China must find ways to feed its growing population.

Government corruption is a large problem. The organization of the Communist Party allows many opportunities for officials to take kickbacks or steal government money. Corrupt officials can appoint the heads of government-owned companies or award government contracts as political favors. Citizens become angry when they see officials living luxurious lifestyles. The government has begun to crack down on corruption within its ranks, especially targeting corrupt executives of government-owned companies.

In addition, China is trying to control the flow of information into and out of the country, mainly via the Internet. Censorship is mainly used to cover up dissent against the government. The government has set up rigid restrictions on Internet access, which has limited the availability of information that Chinese businesses need to grow and develop.

EXECUTIVE BRANCH

The executive branch of the government consists of the president, the vice president, and the State Council, or cabinet. The president is the head of state—the Chinese representative to the rest of the world. The president and vice president are not elected by the people of China in a general election. Rather, they are elected by the legislative branch of the government, called the National People's Congress (NPC). The president and vice president are elected separately, and each can serve two five-year terms. The president reports to the NPC. Hu Jintao was elected president in 2003, and Xi Jinping was elected vice president in 2008.

The State Council runs the government. As China's highest executive agency, it carries out the policies of the Chinese Communist Party and implements all the nation's laws. The head of the State Council is the premier. Under the premier are four vice premiers, five state councillors, and the secretary general. The State Council supervises 26 ministries and commissions, such as national defense, public security, and public health.

Since 2003, the premier has been Wen Jiabao. Since 2008, the executive vice premier has been Le Keqiang. Zhang Dejiang and Wang

STRUCTURE OF THE GOVERNMENT OF CHINA

Legislative	Executive	Judicial	Chinese Communist Party
National People's Congress	President Vice President State Council	Supreme People's Court Local people's Court Special Courts	National Congress Central Committee Chinese People's Political Consultative Conference (CPPCC)

Current president Hu Jintao was elected in 2003 by the National People's Congress, and again for a second term in 2008.

Qishan have been vice premiers since 2008, and Hui Liangyu has been a vice premiere since 2003.

The Chinese national anthem was originally the theme song from a 1935 movie.

LEGISLATIVE BRANCH

The legislative branch of the Chinese government consists of a single body, the NPC. Members of the NPC are elected by other officials in the municipal, regional, and provincial governments and from the armed forces. The NPC has more than 2,900 members, and they serve five-year terms.

The entire NPC meets annually in March or April for several weeks. A smaller Standing Committee meets when the NPC is not in session, and it consists of a chairman, 15 vice chairmen, a secretary general, and 153 members. The duties of the NPC include amending and enforcing the constitution, electing the president and vice president, and examining and approving the nation's economic and social development plans.

The NPC does not draft legislation, however. The Chinese Communist Party and executive branch propose laws, which the NPC then approves. Occasionally, a few members of the NPC vote against a piece of legislation, but most never do. For this reason, some people in the West call the NPC a "rubber stamp" legislature.

JUDICIAL BRANCH

Unlike the judicial branch in the United States, the judicial branch in China does not serve as a check on the other two branches of government, nor does it determine whether new laws are permitted by the constitution. Those responsibilities go to the legislature and

HONG KONG AND MACAU

From 1842 until 1997, Hong Kong was a colony of the United Kingdom. Under British rule, it grew into a modern, skyscraper-filled metropolis. When the British agreed to give Hong Kong back to China, it did so with the assurance that China would retain the capitalistic lifestyle in Hong Kong until 2047. In 1999, China did the same thing with the Portuguese peninsula of Macau. Now, both have some independence from China, with separate governments, legal systems, and laws. However, they come under Chinese rule for foreign affairs and national security.

the Chinese Communist Party. Instead, the judicial branch works with police and prosecutors to make sure the nation's laws and regulations are carried out. Leaders of the Chinese Communist Party can comment on the verdicts of judges and even revise them.

The courts in China consist of the Supreme People's Court, the Local People's Courts, and the Special Courts. The Supreme People's Court is located in Beijing and supervises the other courts; its members are appointed by the NPC. The Local People's Courts are located in provinces, autonomous regions, and special municipalities, and the Special Courts rule on military, maritime, railway, and forestry laws.

LOCAL GOVERNMENTS

China is divided into 23 provinces, five autonomous regions, and four municipalities. Governors are the leaders of the provinces and autonomous regions, while mayors are the leaders of the municipalities.

The individuals in all of these positions are appointed by the central government in Beijing and approved by the NPC.

Below the province level, China is divided into prefectures, which are then divided into counties and cities. The counties are divided into townships and towns, which are then divided into villages. Most of the leaders of these regions are appointed to their positions, but some townships and villages hold elections.

CHINESE COMMUNIST PARTY

China has one ruling political party, the Chinese Communist Party (CCP), and eight smaller parties that are controlled by the CCP. The CCP has

TAIWAN

Since Chiang Kai-shek fled to Taiwan with the Nationalist Party in 1949 and declared it the Republic of China, relations between Taiwan and China have been strained. For a period after World War II, Beijing did not have the military power to regain control of Taiwan, and Taiwan remained under control of the Nationalist government. With the support of the United States, Taiwan grew economically and established a democratic government. Even so, China continued to fight for reunification, and finally, in 2005, it was able to formally end the conflict between the Communists and the Nationalists.

Today, China and Taiwan communicate about economic and diplomatic issues, but they still do not agree on the status of Taiwan. China considers Taiwan a part of the People's Republic of China and even counts Taiwan as one of its provinces. Taiwan, however, still considers itself a separate country.

永 远 跟 党 走

Students create the Chinese Communist Party emblem in honor of joining the youth league.

76 million members.[2] It sets the country's policies, and the national government carries them out.

To do this, the CCP has set up a parallel bureaucracy. This means that for every agency and department in the state government, there is one in the CCP too, allowing it to control the government at all levels. The CCP also makes sure that all key positions in the national government are occupied by leaders of the CCP. And if the CCP needs to enforce its policies, it has the country's main military body, the People's Liberation Army (PLA), at its disposal.

The CCP's National Congress is the highest agency in the party, and it meets once every five years. The National Congress elects a Central Committee, which in turn elects and approves the Political Bureau and the exclusive Standing Committee. The Standing Committee makes most of the decisions for the CCP. The Standing Committee has nine members, including the president of the country and the CCP general secretary— the most powerful position in the party. Often the president and the general secretary are the same person. Hu Jintao currently holds both positions.

The CCP also receives guidance from the Chinese People's Political Consultative Conference (CPPCC). The CPPCC advises the CCP, the state organizations, and other social and political agencies in China. Its members include scholars, educators, intellectuals, and religious leaders. The CPPCC meets once a year.

CONSTITUTION

China's constitution was ratified on December 4, 1982, and amended in 1988, 1993, 1999, and 2004. Article 1 describes China as a "socialist state under the people's democratic dictatorship led by the working class and based on the alliance of workers and peasants."[3] It gives the NPC legislative power and the State Council executive power. It also specifies how provinces, counties, and other local jurisdictions are divided and what authority each government level has.

The constitution allows people 18 years of age and older to vote on members of the NPC up to the county level. From there, delegates elect members for the next-highest level of government, those delegates elect members for the next level, and so on. The constitution also provides for basic human rights, including due process under the law, freedom of religious belief, freedom of assembly, and freedom of speech. However, allowing the Chinese to exercise these rights without interference from the government remains an ongoing issue, as people's rights are often ignored and individuals are punished for political dissent.

Protesters in Hong Kong displayed posters showing imprisoned dissidents in May 2011.

sparse, there are many hydroelectric plants. The Three Gorges Dam project, completed in 2006, is the largest constructed dam in the world.

CHIEF INDUSTRIES

Industry and construction account for almost half of China's GDP, or the amount of wealth and goods produced in the country in a year.[7] Although many smaller industries are moving toward private ownership, the metallurgical and machine industries are still mainly state owned because of their importance to the economy. They account for two-fifths of the total value of industrial output.[8] However, because

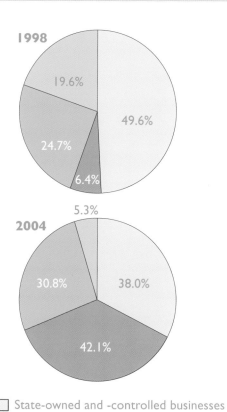

OWNERSHIP OF INDUSTRY[9]

1998
- 49.6%
- 6.4%
- 24.7%
- 19.6%

2004
- 5.3%
- 38.0%
- 42.1%
- 30.8%

- State-owned and -controlled businesses
- Joint-stock corporations
- Foreign-invested businesses
- Collectives

total production is stressed over improving quality and increasing variety, these Chinese industries have been slow to innovate.

Chinese industry includes mining and ore processing, such as iron, steel, aluminum, coal, and petroleum. It also includes manufacturing of automobiles, rail cars, ships, and aircraft. Consumer products such as textiles, clothing, toys, food, and electronics account for a large portion of China's industry.

TOURISM

Since China began opening up to the West in the 1970s, it has become a major attraction for tourists. In 2005, approximately 20 million people traveled to China, and they spent approximately $30 billion.[10] The United Nations World Tourism Organization has predicted that by 2015, China will be one of the world's top destinations for travelers.

China is predicted to become the world's most popular tourist destination by 2020.

Each year, approximately 100 million people visit mainland China from Hong Kong, Macau, and Taiwan, and more than half of all visitors to China come from other Asian countries.[11] Most people visit China's eastern provinces, where they see popular sites such as the Forbidden City, the Great Wall of China, and the terra-cotta warriors at Xi'an.

AGRICULTURE

During the rule of Mao Zedong, farms were turned into large collectives and run by entire villages. Beginning in 1978, the government divided the land into small plots for families to run on their own. Over time, the government loosened its control over agriculture and allowed farmers to set their own prices, decide which crops to plant, and keep their own profits. Today, there are approximately 200 million of these small farms, and they provide food for most of the country.[12]

For the most part, these small farms do not use machinery to harvest crops. Mao encouraged human labor over machine power, and even today most farmers cannot afford machinery. Human power works fairly well for harvesting fruits and vegetables, but it is inefficient for grains and oilseeds, such as sesame seeds. In addition, hundreds of millions of workers have left the farms to seek opportunities in the cities,

RICE

Chinese farmers began growing rice in the south in about 10,000 BCE. Several thousand years passed, however, before they discovered the technique of planting rice in flooded fields, or paddies. This technique requires a great deal of irrigation but produces a much larger crop. Farmers fill low mud banks with water, carefully controlling the level to about 6 inches (15 cm). Ever practical, some farmers even raise fish in the water. Today, farmers throughout China grow rice, producing approximately 35 percent of the world's total supply.[13]

The name for Chinese currency is renminbi, or "people's currency."

CHAPTER 9
CHINA TODAY

For young people in China, life is filled with pressure: pressure to get good grades so they can get into college, pressure to get a good job so they can succeed in a career. And since the implementation of China's policy of one child per family, youth also face pressure to take care of their aging parents, who have made big sacrifices for their only children. Most Chinese youth do not have siblings with whom to share this responsibility.

Thirteen-year-old Gao Yilan starts his day with a breakfast of bread and milk and then rides his bicycle to school at 6:30 a.m. When school ends at 5:15 p.m., he rides back home to the small apartment in Beijing where he lives with his parents, grandmother, and two yellow parrots. Like many Chinese children, Yilan has an English name. It's Seven Eleven because he was born on July 11, or 7/11.

China's policy of one child per family has put today's youth in a position of great responsibility.

Ten-year-old Zhou Yiaying—or Bella, as she's called by her English name—puts in a long day at school and then must complete homework, dinner, and piano practice. Like most Chinese students, she spends approximately five hours a day doing homework. After that, if Bella is allowed to watch TV, she must watch the news. Every Saturday, she takes a prep class for her middle school entrance exams.

Bella and Seven Eleven are lucky because they live with middle-class families. Yu Wang, however, is not so lucky. He lives in a poor section of Hohhot. Because the milk ration provided by the government is so small, Wang's father bought a sheep that he keeps in the country. Every day, the father bicycles 40 minutes so he can bring back fresh milk for the family. Besides studying, Wang takes piano, painting, guitar, and dance classes. His parents struggle to raise the money to provide these classes for their son.

EDUCATION

China's rate of literacy is 91.6 percent.

Approximately 450 million students attend school in China.[1] Some begin in preschool, but most start in elementary school, which goes from age six until sixth grade. After that, four out of every five students take an admission test in the hope of attending middle school. And after that, two out of five middle school students take another admission test to get into high school. Depending on their interests, they may attend an academic school or a vocational school.

Society and families place strong pressure on youth to excel starting at a very young age.

Basic skills such as math and reading are emphasized in Chinese schools over the arts. If students wish to study art, they have to take a class after school. Teachers' primary method of instruction is to require rote memorization, and students commonly have to recite memorized passages in class. As a result, many students graduate with strong memorization skills but weak creative and analytical skills.

For students who wish to go to a college or university, admission is extremely competitive. Each year, the approximately 100 million young people of college age compete for fewer than 20 million openings in colleges and universities.[2] To improve their chances of being admitted, high school students put in 14-hour school days. To lower the stress on young people, the government stopped requiring students to attend weekend, evening, and

SCHOOL ENROLLMENT

Students enrolled in elementary school	99%
Students enrolled in middle school	98%
Students enrolled in high school	23%
Students enrolled in college or university	23%
Students enrolled in graduate school	1.2 million[3]

vacation classes and forbid teachers to assign written homework to first- and second-graders.

CURRENT CHALLENGES

China is a very different country today than it was in the 1960s at the height of Mao Zedong's power. Today, people in China can choose where to work. They can practice their own religion, with some limitations. They can read some books that propose radical ideas about the government, and they can participate in democratic elections at the local level. Economically, China has become one of the most successful countries in the world, and the standard of living for most people continues to improve.

Nonetheless, China has many problems, including environmental damage, lack of fertile farmland, government corruption, economic inequality of migrant workers, and human rights violations. These violations have drawn particular attention, because they involve many rights that people in the Western world take for granted, such as freedom of speech.

And although freedom of speech has improved since the time Mao Zedong ruled, the flow of information in China is still restricted, and people who speak out may face severe punishment. In 1998, the people who tried to form the China Democracy Party were convicted of opposing the government and received long prison sentences. In 2004, more than 20 people were killed while protesting land seizures near

Guangzhou.[4] And in 2010, Nobel Peace Prize winner Liu Xiaobo was unable to attend the award ceremony because he was serving an 11-year prison term for speaking out against the government.

USING THE INTERNET

Although approximately 389 million people have Internet access in China, that access has specific limitations.[5] A system of filters referred to as the "Great Firewall of China" blocks access to Web sites and topics deemed unacceptable. For instance, searching on the topic "Falun Gong"—a religious movement from the 1990s that was banned by the government—would likely produce an error message. Users' access is restricted by thousands of volunteers who search for inappropriate words in e-mails, bulletin boards, blogs, and social networking sites and then filter out the unacceptable text. Cell phones are also subject to oversight. Providers must install filtering equipment that automatically deletes text messages containing unacceptable words. Even so, many young Chinese people have become clever at finding ways to work around the cyber censors and gain wider access to the Internet.

FUTURE OUTLOOK

As China moves into the future, it will most likely continue growing economically—possibly tying or even surpassing the United States for the world's highest GDP. But because China's per capita income is lower than that of most modern countries, it will probably remain a poor country for many years.

Will China ever become a democratic nation? Thousands of small, local protests occur in the country every year. Many experts believe that if these

Supporters of Liu Xiaobo, who was jailed for speaking out against the Chinese government, protest for his release.

groups of protestors organized, they could lead a democratic movement. Experts also believe that the information provided by the Internet could encourage people to insist on a new form of government or that the growth of the Chinese middle class might result in demands for a new government.

The fact that none of these things has happened so far points to the strength of the Chinese Communist Party in both putting down opposition and in meeting the needs of the nation's growing population. Overall, China is a developing nation that views an improving standard of living as a more important human right than the freedoms of speech and religion. And to that end, China is moving forward to improve the lives of its citizens and end poverty in the country.

As ancient and modern customs and standards continue to merge, China looks to the future as a growing nation full of intrigue and possibility.

[TIMELINE]

1600–1000s BCE	The Shang rule China as the first dynasty.
221–206 BCE	The Qin dynasty rules and creates the Great Wall of China.
206 BCE–220 CE	The Han rule as one of China's longest dynasties.
618–907	The Tang dynasty encourages art and religion to flourish.
960–1279	The Song dynasty brings peace and prosperity to southern China.
1279–1368	The Mongols conquer China and form the Yüan dynasty.
1368–1644	The Ming dynasty restores Chinese rule.
1644	The Manchu invade China and form the Qing dynasty.
1839–1842	During the first Opium War, China battles Great Britain over trade.
1857	China battles Great Britain and France in the second Opium War.
1898–1901	In the Boxer Rebellion, Chinese rebels try to expel all foreigners from the nation, resulting in a violent siege in Beijing.
1908	On November 14, Qing Emperor Guangxu dies. On November 15, Empress Dowager Cixi dies and three-year-old Puyi is installed as child emperor.

1912	In February, the Qing dynasty collapses and imperial China ends.
1921	In July, the Chinese Communist Party (CCP) is formed.
1925	On March 12, Sun Yat-sen, leader of the Nationalist Party, dies, and General Chiang Kai-shek becomes the new leader.
1934–1935	Mao Zedong's Communists retreat from the Nationalist army across China in the Long March.
1949	On October 1, Mao Zedong forms the People's Republic of China in Beijing. The Nationalists retreat to Taiwan.
1958	The Great Leap Forward movement is launched with the goal of modernizing China, but mass starvation results.
1966–1976	Mao Zedong tries to transform society with the Cultural Revolution.
1982	China's current constitution is ratified on December 4.
1989	Student protests in Tiananmen Square in Beijing are put down by the Chinese military, resulting in hundreds of deaths.
1997	On July 1, Hong Kong becomes a special administrative region of China, ending British rule of the city.
1999	On December 20, Macau becomes a special administrative region after 400 years under Portuguese rule.
2008	China hosts the Summer Olympic Games in Beijing.

FACTS AT YOUR FINGERTIPS

GEOGRAPHY

Official name: People's Republic of China (PRC) (in Chinese, Zhonghua Renmin Gongheguo)

Area: 3,705,407 square miles (9,596,961 sq km)

Climate: A monsoon climate with a dry fall, winter, and spring and a rainy summer

Highest elevation: Mount Everest, 29,035 feet (8,850 m) above sea level

Lowest elevation: Turfan Depression, 508 feet (155 m) below sea level

Significant geographic features: Himalayas, Great Wall of China, Yangtze River

PEOPLE

Population (July 2011 est.): 1,336,718,015

Most populous city: Shanghai

Ethnic groups: Han, 91.5 percent; ethnic minorities, 8 percent (Zhuang, Manchu, Hui, Yao, Uighur, Mongol, Tibetan, Buyei, Korean)

Percentage of residents living in urban areas: 47 percent (2010)

Life expectancy: 74.68 years at birth (world rank: 96)

Language(s): Standard Chinese or Mandarin (Putonghua, based on Beijing dialect), Yue (Cantonese), Wu (Shanghainese), Minbei (Fuzhou), Minnan (Hokkien-Taiwanese), Xian, Gan, Hakka dialects, minority languages

Religion(s): China is officially atheist; Taoism, Buddhism, and Christianity, 3 to 4 percent; Islam, 1 to 2 percent

GOVERNMENT AND ECONOMY

Government: Communist state

Capital: Beijing

Date of adoption of current constitution: December 4, 1982, with amendments in 1988, 1993, 1999, 2004

Head of state: president

Head of government: premier

Legislature: National People's Congress

Currency: renminbi

Industries and natural resources: iron, steel, aluminum, and other metals; coal; machine building; armaments; textiles and apparel; petroleum; cement; chemicals; fertilizers; consumer products, including footwear, toys, and electronics; food processing; transportation equipment, telecommunications equipment, commercial space launch vehicles, and satellites

NATIONAL SYMBOLS

Holiday: A national holiday on October 1 celebrates the founding of the People's Republic of China.

Flag: Red with a large, yellow, five-pointed star and four small, yellow, five-pointed stars

National anthem: "Yiyonggjun Jinxingqu" ("The March of the Volunteers")

National animal: None; the giant panda and dragon are common symbols

KEY PEOPLE

Emperor Shihuangdi (259–210 BCE) of the Qin dynasty, initiated work on the Great Wall

Genghis Kahn and the Mongols (1200s), invaded China and formed the Yüan dynasty

Sun Yat-sen (1866–1925), formed the Nationalist Party and is considered the father of modern China

Mao Zedong (1893–1976), served as the first leader of the Chinese Communist Party (CCP)

Deng Xiaoping (1904–1997), served as the first Communist leader after Mao and began a series of reforms.

PROVINCES AND OTHER TERRITORIES IN CHINA

Province; Capital

Anhui; Heifei

Fujian; Fuzhou

Gansu; Lanzhou

Guangdong; Guangzhou

Guizhou; Guiyang

Hainan; Haikou

Hebei; Shijiazhuang

Heilongjiang; Harbin

Henan; Zengzhou

Hubei; Wuhan

Hunan; Changsha

Jiangsu; Nanjing

Jiangxi; Nanchang

Jilin; Changhun

Liaoning; Shenyang

Qinghai; Xining

Shaanxi; Xi'an

Shandong; Jinan

Shanxi; Taiyuan

Sichuan; Chengdu

Yunnan; Kunming

Zhejiang; Hangzhou

(Taiwan; Taipei)

Autonomous Region; Capital

Guangxi; Nanning

Inner Mongolia; Hohhot

Ningxia; Yinchuan

Tibet; Lhasa

Xinjiang; Ürümqi

Municipalities

Beijing

Chongqing

Shanghai

Tianjin

Special Administrative Region; Administrative Center

Hong Kong; Victoria

Macau; Macau City

GLOSSARY

arable
Fertile and fit for agriculture.

assimilate
To integrate into a new culture.

bureaucracy
A system of administration in which agencies and departments are staffed by nonelected officials.

communism
An economic system defined by collective ownership of property and the organization of labor for common advantage; a government system in which a single party holds power and the state controls the economy.

concubine
A woman who is the official mistress of a wealthy married man but has some of the social status of a wife.

dowager
A widow who has inherited a title and property from her husband.

dynasty
A succession of rulers from the same family or line.

firewall
A form of security software intended to prevent unauthorized access to a computer's software or data.

gross domestic product

A measure of a country's economy; the total of all goods and services produced in a country in a year.

imperial

Relating to an empire or its ruler.

loess

The fine-grained, yellowish-brown deposit of soil left by the wind.

migrant

A person who moves from one place to another, often to seek a better job or lifestyle.

monsoon

A large-scale wind system that seasonally blows in opposite directions and affects the climate of a region.

reparations

Paying money for repairs, especially after war.

socialism

An economic system in which the government controls the means of production and distribution of goods.

topography

The physical and natural features of an area.

ADDITIONAL RESOURCES

SELECTED BIBLIOGRAPHY

DK Eyewitness Travel Guides: China. New York: Dorling Kindersley, 2005. Print.

Fenby, Jonathan, ed. *The Seventy Wonders of China.* New York: Thames & Hudson, 2007. Print.

National Geographic Atlas of China. Washington, DC: National Geographic Society, 2008. Print.

Starr, John Bryan. *Understanding China.* New York: Hill and Wang, 2010. Print.

Waserstrom, Jeffrey, N. *China in the 21st Century, What Everyone Needs to Know.* Oxford, Eng.: Oxford UP, 2010. Print.

FURTHER READINGS

Chang, Leslie T. *Factory Girls: From Village to City in a Changing China.* New York: Spiegel & Grau, 2009. Print.

Hessler, Peter. *River Town: Two Years on the Yangtze.* New York: Harper Perennial, 2006. Print.

Spurling, Hilary. *Pearl Buck in China: Journey to the Good Earth.* New York: Simon & Schuster, 2010. Print.

WEB SITES

To learn more about China, visit ABDO Publishing Company online at **www.abdopublishing.com**. Web sites about China are featured on our Book Links page. These links are routinely monitored and updated to provide the most current information available.

PLACES TO VISIT

If you are ever in China, consider checking out these important and interesting sites!

The Great Wall of China

Begun in the Qin dynasty and continued in the Ming dynasty, this wall is the world's largest military structure. It can be accessed in various spots throughout China, but most visitors access it in the Badaling section near Beijing.

Museum of the Terra-Cotta Warriors and Horses of Shihuangdi

This archaeological site and museum in Xi'an houses thousands of terra-cotta warriors that were buried with the first emperor of the Qin dynasty.

The Palace Museum

The Palace Museum in Beijing is a complex that includes the Forbidden City—the palace occupied by Chinese emperors from the Ming through Qing dynasties—along with an art museum that houses a vast collection of artwork.

SOURCE NOTES

CHAPTER 1. A VISIT TO CHINA

1. *DK Eyewitness Travel Guides: China.* New York: Dorling Kindersley, 2005. Print. 87.

2. "China's Great Wall Far Longer Than Thought: Survey." *Sydney Morning Herald.* Fairfax Media, 20 Apr. 2009. Web. 13 Dec. 2010.

3. Simon Foster, et al. *Frommer's China.* New Jersey: Wiley, 2008. Print. 266.

4. *DK Eyewitness Travel Guides: China.* New York: Dorling Kindersley, 2005. Print. 16.

CHAPTER 2. GEOGRAPHY: LAND OF CONTRASTS

1. "Country Profile: China." *Library of Congress.* Library of Congress, Federal Research Division, Aug. 2006. Web. 29 Jan. 2011.

2. "The World Factbook: China." *Central Intelligence Agency.* Central Intelligence Agency, 7 Dec. 2010. Web. 1 Dec. 2010.

3. *DK Eyewitness Travel Guides: China.* New York: Dorling Kindersley, 2005. Print. 20.

4. "China." *Encyclopædia Britannica.* Encyclopædia Britannica, 2011. Web. 30 Jan. 2011.

5. "Yangtze River." *Encyclopædia Britannica.* Encyclopædia Britannica, 2011. Web. 30 Jan. 2011.

6. "Huang He." *Encyclopædia Britannica.* Encyclopædia Britannica, 2011. Web. 30 Jan. 2011.

7. *National Geographic Atlas of China.* Washington, DC: National Geographic Society, 2008. Print. 36.

8. Jonathan Fenby. *The Seventy Wonders of China.* New York: Thames & Hudson, 2007. Print. 37.

9. "Country Guide: China." *BBC: Weather.* BBC, n.d. Web. 31 Jan. 2011.

10. Stephen G. Haw. *A Traveller's History of China.* New York: Interlink, 1995. Print. 22.

CHAPTER 3. ANIMALS AND NATURE: DIVERSITY OF LIFE

1. *National Geographic Atlas of China.* Washington, DC: National Geographic Society, 2008. Print. 40.

2. Damian Harper. *China.* Oakland, CA: Lonely Planet, 2009. Print. 101.

3. "Summary Statistics: Summaries by Country, Table 5, Threatened Species in Each Country." *IUCN Red List of Threatened Species.* International Union for Conservation of Nature and Natural Resources, 2010. Web. 18 Jan. 2011.

4. Damian Harper. *China.* Oakland, CA: Lonely Planet, 2009. Print. 102.

5. Ibid. 98.

6. Michelle Nijhuis. "Bamboo Boom: Is This the Material for You?" *Scientific American*. Scientific American, 20 July 2009. Web. 4 Jan. 2011.

7. *DK Eyewitness Travel Guides: China.* New York: Dorling Kindersley, 2005. Print. 217.

8. *National Geographic Atlas of China.* Washington, DC: National Geographic Society, 2008. Print. 43.

9. Ibid. 42.

10. "Ailuropoda melanoleuca Giant Panda." *IUCN Red List of Threatened Species.* International Union for Conservation of Nature and Natural Resources, n.d. Web. 15. Mar. 2011.

11. *National Geographic Atlas of China.* Washington, DC: National Geographic Society, 2008. Print. 44–45.

CHAPTER 4. HISTORY: THE OLDEST CIVILIZATION

1. "Taiping Rebellion." *Encyclopædia Britannica.* Encyclopædia Britannica, 2011. Web. 30 Jan. 2011.

2. "Long March." *Encyclopædia Britannica.* Encyclopædia Britannica, 2011. Web. 30 Jan. 2011.

CHAPTER 5. PEOPLE: PROUD TRADITIONS

1. "The World Factbook: China." *Central Intelligence Agency.* Central Intelligence Agency, 7 Dec. 2010. Web. 1 Dec. 2010.

2. *National Geographic Atlas of China.* Washington, DC: National Geographic Society, 2008. Print. 46.

3. John Bryan Starr. *Understanding China.* New York: Hill and Wang, 2010. Print. 29.

4. "The World Factbook: China." *Central Intelligence Agency.* Central Intelligence Agency, 7 Dec. 2010. Web. 1 Dec. 2010.

5. *National Geographic Atlas of China.* Washington, DC: National Geographic Society, 2008. Print. 47.

6. "The World Factbook: China." *Central Intelligence Agency.* Central Intelligence Agency, 7 Dec. 2010. Web. 1 Dec. 2010.

7. Ibid

8. John Bryan Starr. *Understanding China.* New York: Hill and Wang, 2010. Print. 33.

9. Jonathan Fenby. *The Seventy Wonders of China.* New York: Thames & Hudson, 2007. Print. 80.

SOURCE NOTES CONTINUED

10. "Background Note: China." *US Department of State.* US Department of State, 5 Aug. 2010. Web. 16 Jan. 2011.

11. *DK Eyewitness Travel Guides: China.* New York: Dorling Kindersley, 2005. Print. 26.

12. "Backgrounder: Religion in China." *Council on Foreign Relations.* Council on Foreign Relations, 16 May 2008. Web. 14 Apr. 2011.

13. Damian Harper. *China.* Oakland, CA: Lonely Planet, 2009. Print. 65.

CHAPTER 6. CULTURE: A RICH HERITAGE

1. Damian Harper. *China.* Oakland, CA: Lonely Planet, 2009. Print. 70.

2. Ibid. 79.

3. Ibid. 74.

4. Stephen Cook. "The Tallest Buildings in the World." *Washington Post.* Washington Post, 4 Jan. 2010. Web. 16 Mar. 2011.

CHAPTER 7. POLITICS: A MULTILAYERED SYSTEM

1. *National Geographic Atlas of China.* Washington, DC: National Geographic Society, 2008. Print. 48.

2. "Background Note: China." *US Department of State.* US Department of State, 5 Aug. 2010. Web. 16 Jan. 2011.

3. *The Central People's Government of the People's Republic of China.* www.gov.cn.english, 2006. Web. 30 Jan. 2011.

CHAPTER 8. ECONOMICS: RISING STAR

1. *National Geographic Atlas of China.* Washington, DC: National Geographic Society, 2008. Print. 58.

2. "The World Factbook: China." *Central Intelligence Agency.* Central Intelligence Agency, 12 Jan. 2011. Web. 30 Jan. 2011.

3. Ibid.

4. "Country Profile: China." *Library of Congress.* Library of Congress, Federal Research Division, Aug. 2006. Web. 29 Jan. 2011.

5. "China." *Encyclopædia Britannica.* Encyclopædia Britannica, 2011. Web. 30 Jan. 2011.

6. *DK Eyewitness Travel Guides: China*. New York: Dorling Kindersley, 2005. Print. 268.

7. "Background Note: *China.*" *US Department of State*. US Department of State, 5. Aug. 2010. Web. 16 Jan. 2011.

8. "China." *Encyclopædia Britannica*. Encyclopædia Britannica, 2011. Web. 30 Jan. 2011.

9. John Bryan Starr. *Understanding China*. New York: Hill and Wang, 2010. Print. 148.

10. *National Geographic Atlas of China*. Washington, DC: National Geographic Society, 2008. Print. 56.

11. Ibid. 57.

12. Ibid. 62.

13. *DK Eyewitness Travel Guides: China*. New York: Dorling Kindersley, 2005. Print. 280.

14. "China." *Encyclopædia Britannica*. Encyclopædia Britannica, 2011. Web. 30 Jan. 2011.

15. Ibid.

16. *National Geographic Atlas of China*. Washington, DC: National Geographic Society, 2008. Print. 66.

17. Ibid. 60.

18. "The World Factbook: China." *Central Intelligence Agency*. Central Intelligence Agency, 8 Mar. 2011. Web. 17 Mar. 2011.

19. Ibid.

20. Stephen A. Leibo. *East and Southeast Asia*. Harpers Ferry, WV: Stryker-Post, 2008. Print. 33.

21. John Bryan Starr. *Understanding China*. New York: Hill and Wang, 2010. Print. 103.

CHAPTER 9. CHINA TODAY

1. John Bryan Starr. *Understanding China*. New York: Hill and Wang, 2010. Print. 262.

2. Ibid.

3. John Bryan Starr. *Understanding China*. New York: Hill and Wang, 2010. Print. 267.

4. Joseph Kahn. "Military Officer Tied to Killings Is Held by China." *New York Times*. New York Times, 12 Dec. 2005. Web. 8 Mar. 2011.

5. "The World Factbook: China." *Central Intelligence Agency*. Central Intelligence Agency, 12 Jan. 2011. Web. 30 Jan. 2011.

INDEX

PHOTO CREDITS

Shutterstock Images, cover, 2, 37, 88, 97, 129 (bottom); George Clerk/iStockphoto, 5 (top), 11, 130; Hung Chung Chih/Shutterstock Images, 5 (middle), 28, 131; Ariadna de Raadt/Shutterstock Images, 5 (bottom), 127; Songquan Deng/Dreamstime, 6; Bigstock, 9, 16; Matt Kania/Map Hero, Inc., 12, 19, 23, 61, 115; Zhu Difeng/Shutterstock Images, 21; Fotolia, 26, 117; iStockphoto, 31, 104; Morales Morales/Photolibrary, 33; G Dagli Orti/Photolibrary, 40; Daniel Padavona/ Shutterstock Images, 43, 128 (top); Bridgeman Art Library/Getty Images, 46; Museum of East Asian Art/Photolibrary, 49; World History Archive/Alamy, 51; AP Images, 54, 129 (top); Peter Scholey/Photolibrary, 56; Dreamstime, 58; Alex Mares-Manton/Photolibrary, 62; Norbert Michalke/Photolibrary, 65; Roman Sigaev/iStockphoto, 69; Tamir Niv/Shutterstock Images, 73; Eastphoto/Photolibrary, 74; Robert Paul Van Beets/Shutterstock Images, 77; Bartlomiej Magierowski/Shutterstock Images, 79; Yvonne Bogdanski/Dreamstime, 81; Cao Ji/Imaginechina/ AP Images, 85; Alex Nikada/iStockphoto, 90, 132; Ng Han Guan/AP Images, 95; STR/AP Images, 100; Vincent Yu/AP Images, 103; Du Huaju/AP Images, 108; Chun-Tso Lin/Shutterstock Images, 112; View Stock/Photolibrary, 118; Peng Nian/Imaginechina/AP Images, 121; Kin Cheung/AP Images, 125